Albion

An introduction to the
new beadwork stitch

Heather Kingsley-Heath

Published by
The Useful Booklet Company
P.O. Box 2394
Radstock, Somerset
BA3 3WL United Kingdom.

ISBN: 0-9543672-7-8

Author: Heather Kingsley-Heath

Printed in Great Britain
Bath Midway Litho Ltd
Trowbridge, Wiltshire.

The Useful Booklet Company
publishes books about beadwork.
There are five beginners' guide booklets:
Beaded Earrings
Loom Weaving
Beaded Mandalas
Christmas Decorations
Buttons and Beads.

The Useful Booklet Company is also
dedicated to supporting the Minerva
Beaders who raise funds for two
primary schools in a remote area of
Zimbabwe. The story and lots of great
beading projects are available in the
hugely popular book, Minerva Spirals.
Proceeds from the sale of the book
go directly to the fund.

All these, plus other titles written by
Heather, are available on her website at:
www.heatherworks.co.uk

Thanks and praise

Beadwork is an art form and an absorbing and creative hobby
resulting in delicious adornment and affordable treasure.
It has been the currency of global trade. The expression of cultural identity.
It is a decorative language in which the narrative has no boundaries
and no ending. To this great mix I add my own small story.

In the preparation of this book I have many people to thank:

First and always, himself, for keeping our boat afloat, for quietly being
the best, and almost never resenting the time I spend with my beads.

My friends Sally Plummer and Dawn Toms for their enthusiasm,
constant encouragement and the genuine gift of friendship.

My friend and art buddy Caroline, who happily throws me a curve ball
when I'm getting too precious, is never afraid to be honest
and who always dares me to be greater than I believe I can be.

My many students who come to my workshops, you are a constant
source of inspiration, laughter and fun. Keep it real girls.

To Mike and Helen at Bath Midway Litho Ltd. We work together often
and even in a crisis it is fun For your enthusiasm, energy
and impromptu lunches, I thank you.

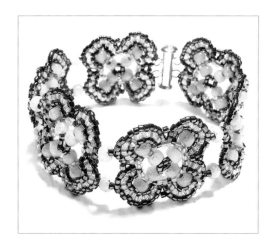

Introduction

Beadwork, those millions of tiny pieces of glass capture my attention.
I love colour and texture and my inspiration comes from everywhere, a
snippet of history, the sound of bird song while I'm gardening, two colours
that just have to dance together or a piece of vintage loveliness.

Carl Jung wrote, 'The creative mind plays with the objects it loves.'
Playing with a new idea is like a creative treasure hunt for me, which is
what led to the development of Albion Stitch. As I worked I realised
that this simple stitch fulfilled many criteria. It is ideal for beginners as a
learning tool as it is infinitely adaptable in its most simple form.
The stitch can also be intellectually challenging for more experienced
beaders, with enough range to enable a designer to create any object of
his or her desire, whether it be two dimensional or sculptural.

Here in book one, I introduce you to the basics of Albion Stitch and the
logical variations, to show you that it can be many shapes. Each chapter is
a stepping stone to enable you to build a real understanding of the stitch
and to enjoy creating wearable adornments.

The projects are laid out so that you can try the steps in sequence.
You will soon see that with each additional step, there are many variations
which you can wander off and explore. Permit yourself the time to play
at any point; to experiment with bead sizes, colours, counts and stitch
lengths and to develop your own version of a design.

If like me, you discover that this stitch is satisfying to work and you want
to explore it some more, join me again in book two where I show you
how Albion Stitch can be used to create bezels, birds, beetles, containers
and sculptural pieces.

Beadwork is a gentle hobby, it requires time, a little patience and the
willingness to let a day or an afternoon slip by as you work. For me there
is nothing so lovely as the calm that settles when all I have in front of me
is a day of creating and a new design to play with. I hope you will enjoy
exploring Albion Stitch as much as I have creating it for you.

Chapter one 6-9

How to get started: tools, colours, beads and the language of Albion Stitch.

Chapter two 10-13

Inspired by green. Basic flat linear Albion Stitch and project variations.

Chapter three 14-19

Inspired by red. Develop the flat Linear stitch variations.

Chapter four 20-27

Inspired by vintage colours.
Explore the stitch length variations.

Chapter five 28-35

Inspired by natural neutrals. Shape the stitch with flat round variations.

Chapter six 36-43

Inspired by summer colours. Shape the stitch with tubular variations.

Chapter seven 44-52

Inspired by vintage flowers. Extend the shaping to create beaded beads.

Chapter eight 53-63

Inspired by antiqued metal. Shape the stitch with filigree and lace formations.

The projects

Tools and materials

Most of you will already be fellow bead addicts I expect, but if you are a beginner you will need the basic equipment to get started.

Beading thread. There are several brands of thread available in a whole range of colours. Beading threads also come in several thicknesses, 'D' is ideal for size 11° seed beads and for the projects in this book.
I also recommend that you have a spool of 4lb (A) or 6lb (D) Fireline thread. This is a tough nylon thread, versatile enough for you to work beadwork stitches easily, but tough enough to withstand working with crystals and bugle beads which can have sharp edges. It is also a handy thread for stringing beaded beads together.

Needles. Beading needles have an elongated eye, but are the same diameter along the whole length. Beading needles come in several thicknesses '10' is ideal for general beadwork, with thinner '12' or '13' preferable for smaller beads. Beading needles come in several lengths, choose the one that feels right for you.

Scissors. A small pair of sharp scissors are essential. Never cut anything other than your thread with them, never lend them and they will serve you well.

Scoop. Like a miniature shovel, the bead scoop is one of those accessories no beading box should be without. It makes tidying away the beads at the end of a session easy and fun.

Beading mat. Line a tray with a beading mat. Made of material similar to fleece the surface of the beading mat enables you to pick up beads easily and spill out little piles of beads without them rolling about.

Snack breaks. Join any beading group and you will witness multi-tasking at it's best. Gossip, tea drinking and sinful snacks appear to go very well with beading. Never view beading as an excuse not to stop and eat.

More seriously, it is all too easy to get engrossed in a beading project, so please take regular breaks to stretch and move about every so often, to ease your joints and muscles. Take a break to look at the middle distance or horizon, this will help to relax your eyes if you've been beading for a little too long.

Colours and beads

The first delight in becoming a bead addict is the huge array of seed beads, and shopping for them is the grown-up equivalent of buying sweets.
The second delight is sorting though your purchases to create new combinations of colours, although you may find that you will need to go back to buy just the right shade of this or that to be completely satisfied for now!

Throughout the book I've put together different colour combinations and the inspiration for how they were chosen. Many of the images are of either textiles or flowers. Both are part of my everyday life and therefore on hand to use as inspiration.

Within the materials lists I don't give colour codes for the beads I've used because, if you can't source the same beads, I want you to feel free to use any colour mix.
If you wish to exactly replicate the colour mix in my samples, use the photos as a guide.

Most of the seed beads we use are manufactured in Japan by three companies, Miyuki, Matsuno and Toho. All three make uniform beads in a range of sizes.
The other source for seed beads is Czechoslovakia. Czech beads differ slightly from Japanese beads in size and shape so, if you work with Czech seed beads stick with them rather than mixing them with Japanese seed beads.

Seed beads come in a selection of sizes, from 6° through to 15°, with 6° being the largest and 15° the smallest. Size 11° is currently the most commonly used size in beadwork. Size 15° is useful for finer detail within a design. All the projects in this book will call for 11's with the occasional 6°, 8° and 15°.

Cylinder beads are miniature tubes, without the rounded sides of regular seed beads, available in sizes 10°, 11° and 15°. These are used in the filigree project on pages 56 to 63. Substitute round seed beads if you don't have cylinder beads.

Bugle beads are elongated tubes and are available in various lengths given in millimetres. I've used them for the tubular projects on pages 38 to 42 and in the filigree projects.

Cubes and Triangles are shaped as their names suggest. I've used size 10° triangle beads and both 1.8mm and 3mm cubes as accent beads for some of the projects.

Other beads used in the designs are generally called accent beads. I've opted to use Swarovski Crystals which are definitely the fondant creams of bead shopping! Within the book I've used the bicone shape in 4mm size.
I have also used some Czech crystals, sometimes called fire polished. These have a softer shape but are also available in 4mm.

Albion Stitch language

If you are familiar with beadwork techniques you will recognise the elements of Albion Stitch; Picots, strung together through the tips, with the option of a single Peyote Stitch row to create different effects.

As I developed the stitch and began to teach it, I found that a set of simple terms to describe the stitch with its own language was more useful than the brief description above. I use these terms throughout the books to make the instructions for variations and patterns easy to follow.

Albion Stitch components:

Foundation row / Foundation ring
A row of single beads with an even or odd number. For circular and tubular techniques the strand of beads is tied in a ring. For flat techniques a stop bead is used and then removed once the first row is completed.

The Stitch: Stalk and tip
One or more beads form the stalk, a single bead forms the tip. To make the stitch, pass back down through the stalk beads.

Stitch over foundation bead
The placement of the stitch (stalk and tip) is an essential move to keep the foundation row straight and smooth. To 'stitch over', bring the needle through the foundation bead, left to right (or vice versa), create the stalk and tip, pass back through the stalk and back through the foundation bead from left to right (or vice versa). This will anchor the stitch OVER the foundation bead.

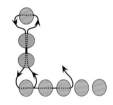

Stitch above foundation bead
Bring the needle through the first foundation bead. Create the stalk and tip, pass back through the stalk and through the third foundation bead. The stitch will sit ABOVE the second foundation bead.

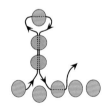

Stitch between foundation beads
Bring the needle through the first foundation bead, create the stitch, then pass into the next foundation bead. The stitch will lie above the space BETWEEN the first and second foundation beads.

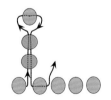

Albion Stitch language

Spacer row

At the end of a completed row of stalk and tip stitches, bring the needle up through the last stalk and tip worked to be in position to make the spacer row.

Pick up a single bead then pass through the next tip bead. Repeat to the end of the row.

The tip and spacer beads now form the base or new foundation row for the next row of Albion Stitch.

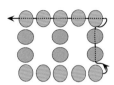

Anchor row

This is a row of single beads placed over alternate beads of the previous row. It can be be worked to place beads over the tip beads, passing through the spacer beads. Or it can be worked to place beads over the spacer beads, passing through the tip beads. It is worked like a Peyote Stitch row but differs in that the beads will stand slightly more 'proud' than in regular Peyote Stitch.

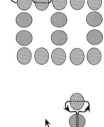

Albion Stitch between anchor row

Place the stalk and tip stitches of the next row to be worked between the beads of the anchor row.

Bring the needle out of an anchor bead, create the stalk and tip, pass back down through the stalk and into the next anchor bead.

The stitch will sit BETWEEN the anchor beads.

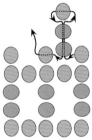

Albion Stitch over anchor row

Bring the needle through the anchor bead, passing from left to right. Create the stalk and tip, pass back through the stalk beads and back through the anchor bead from left to right. Pass through the spacer bead of the row below, then through the next anchor bead, ready to form the next stitch.

The stitch will sit OVER the anchor bead.

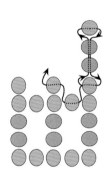

More detail

This is the 'language' , refer back to this page whenever needed. There are still lots of questions to be answered - how to turn at the end of a row, what about thread tension - these and more will be answered as you work through each design.

...green, calm and peaceful.

Inspiration for colour mixes is all around us. Easiest are the greens that abound in nature. Take a walk, pick some leaves and match your beads to the colours.
An old tweed jacket gave me the colour mix for the first project in a delicious mix of spring green shades. The patterns in a garden fence and gate were the inspiration for the very first Albion Stitch experiments.

ingredients...

size 11° seed beads 10g each:
silver lined lime (A)
frosted lime green (B)
frosted aqua (C)
frosted blue green (D)

beading needle

beading thread

clasp of your choice: *or a silver magnetic sliding clasp with 3 loops.*

Foundation row
Use a stop bead (not shown in diagrams), thread on 19 beads, start with silver lined lime green (A) and alternate with frosted lime green (B).

Work the stalk and tip row
Push all the beads down to the stop bead.
Pick up 2xC stalk beads and 1xA tip bead.
Pass back through the stalk 2xC, and through the two beads next to the last foundation bead, 1xB, 1xA.
To pull the thread up tight, hold the tip bead as you pull.

Add another stalk and tip (2xC, 1xA), pass back through the stalk beads and the A bead on the foundation row the thread started from. Pass through two more beads on the foundation row (1xB, 1xA).

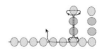

Turn at the end of the row
When there is a stitch over each A bead on the foundation row, remove the stop bead and tie the working thread to the tail. Pass up through the stalk and the tip bead of the last stitch.

Add the spacer row
Pick up 1xB, pass through the next tip bead.
Repeat until the thread is coming out of the tip bead of the first stitch worked at the end of the row.

Add more rows
Work more rows alternating the stalk colours (C and D).
When the piece is long enough for a bracelet, finish with a spacer bead row. Stitch your chosen clasp in place.

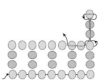

variations to play with...

With even a simple colour palette it is easy to create a whole range of patterns by playing with the sequence of colours and the length of the stitches you use. These first examples of Albion Stitch show how versatile it can be in its most basic form.

project one variations...

Change bead colours, bead sizes, stitch lengths and the number of stitches and Albion Stitch at its most simple can be worked in many combinations.

Vary the stalk lengths

The stalk and tip construction of the stitch can be altered. The design shown far left is worked using a sequence of stalk lengths. Three rows of one bead stalks, followed by two rows of two bead stalks, followed by one row of three bead stalks and back again. To create a 'woven tweed' effect this design uses one colour for all the stalk beads, a second colour for all the tip beads and a third colour for all the spacer beads.

Vary the colour

The design shown centre left is worked throughout with one bead stalks, to form a dense yet still flexible fabric of beads. Pick a range of colours from dark to light for the stalks and spacer bead, and a single unifying colour for the tip beads.
Just playing with colour will give an infinite variety of patterns.

Use all the beads of the foundation row

The design on the right has two variations within it. The stitches sit over each bead of the foundation rows. The stitches also alternate within each row with two size 11° beads for the first stalk, three size 15° beads for the second stalk. All the tip beads are size 11°. This gives a dense fabric as there is only just enough room to accommodate the 15° beads between the size 11° bead stitches. To allow more space use a size 10° or 9° bead for the foundation row and tip beads.

Omit stitches to create spaces

The second variation within the design on the right is the omission of stitches from every fourth row. Because each bead on the base row has a stalk above it, there is no need for a spacer row, simply thread through all the tip beads.

To leave gaps omit the stitches on the chosen foundation row to form the bottom edge of the gap. Thread through the tip beads and add the same number of beads between the tips above the spaces where stitches were omitted. This will give a new foundation row with the correct number of beads to start the next row of stitches.

Change the stitch count

To create a band of Albion Stitch in any width. The foundation row will need to have an odd number of beads (so that the stitch row starts and end with a stitch). Narrow bands make great ribbon like lariats. Create a wider band and fold it, then stitch the edges to form a simple amulet purse.

inspired by the colours...

...mix pink, red and orange.

Mix hot colours like pink, red, scarlet, magenta and orange. Cool the mix with a soft mauve, dove grey or a light warm brown. As always, the texture of the beads adds to the mood. Colour lined and translucent matt keep it gentle, sparkling iridescent and opaque matt finishes spice things up visually.

ingredients...

size 11° seed beads 10g each:

Colour lined magenta (A)

matt orange (B)

matt red (C)

clasp of your choice: *or use a copper coloured sliding clasp with 3 loops.*

Foundation row
Use a stop bead, thread on 13 beads, alternating A and B.

Work the stalk and tip row
Pick up stalk beads 3xC and tip bead 1xA. Pass back through 3xC, and through two beads on the foundation row 1xB, 1xA. Repeat to complete the row.
Remove the stop bead and tie the working thread to the tail. Pass up through the stalk and tip beads of the last stitch.

Add the spacer row, then an anchor bead row
Pick up 1xB, pass through the next tip bead. Repeat to the end of the row. Working back along the spacer row, pick up 1xA, pass through the next spacer (B) bead. Repeat to the end of the row.

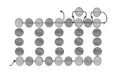

Turn, then work the new row over the anchor beads
Pick up the last anchor bead, tuck the needle under the thread holding the tip bead below, pass back through the anchor bead. Work the first stitch of the new row, pass back through the anchor bead, the next spacer bead and the next anchor bead to be in place to work the next stitch.

Turn at the other end of the row
Work the last stitch of the row, then pass back through the anchor bead, then through the tip bead below it, then through the anchor bead again, and the beads of the last stitch to be in place to start the next spacer bead row.

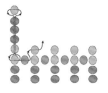

Finishing off
When the piece is a bracelet length, end with a spacer bead row. Stitch your chosen clasp to in place.

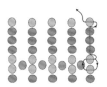

variations to play with...

Project two uses the stitch over anchor bead variation which leaves
the anchor and tip beads with thread showing at the sides.

Embellish the edges

Thread through the stalk beads of one edge, bring the needle
through the tip bead from inner to outer edge, pick up 3x size 15°
beads. Pass through the anchor bead above the tip bead from
outer to inner edge, then pass up through the next set
of stalk beads. This is a simple finishing technique which will
also add strength to the outer edges of your piece.

Adding other beads

The design shown below left is worked with alternating stitch rows,
the first row is worked with 3x11° magenta pink stalks, the second is worked
with 3x11° stalks in a paler shade of pink and 1x4mm crystal stalks worked in at
random. The crystals are pink with a double AB finish to add some sparkle.
All the tip, spacer and anchor beads are worked in a frosted mauve size 11° bead.

The design shown below right is in a more muted colour range. The stalks are
worked as 2x11° frosted coffee and 1x3mm round fire polished coffee coloured
crystal. The anchor and tip beads are worked in size 11° opaque matt rust and the
spacer beads are transparent chocolate. The edging is worked with 1x11°, 1x3mm
crystal, 1x11°. To accommodate the larger beads, the thread is brought out of the
stalk beads and the new beads are added. The thread is passed into the next set of
stalk beads. This bypasses the tip and anchor beads but covers them neatly.

more ideas...

Project three which follows on page 18, uses the stitch between the anchor bead variation and includes a step to cover the edges as you work.

Try other beads
There are many pretty accent beads that can be used instead of crystals. Just make sure they are approximately 4mm diameter to fit within the pattern.
To accommodate longer accent beads, add more beads to the seed bead stalks to achieve the right length of stitch. For a smoother finish try alternating bugle beads, or use bugle beads for every stalk, 4 or 6mm will give you a nice stitch length.

Colour play
If the red, pink, and orange mix is too close for comfort, try adding some new accent colours, purple and lavender work well. A dash of cool yellow will liven things up. If you want to soften the mix further pick out some very pale shades of pink and orange. Cream and pale grey will also give this mix a more gentle effect.

Clasps and closures
Magnetic tube clasps are a neat solution for wider bracelets as they stay done up and are not too intrusive. They are available in a range of metal finishes from silver through to copper and black. Stitch the clasp in place with beading thread.
To hide the thread, make a loop of size 15° beads and pass it through the link of the clasp.

Thread ends and finishing off
To start a new thread, lay the old tail along side the new thread end, take both and form a loop. Pass both tails (old and new) through the loop and tighten the knot, easing it towards your beadwork. With one tail in each hand, tug and the knot will slide down to the beadwork. Continue working with the new thread, then go back and weave the thread tails into your beadwork and snip off the ends.

Tension
Thread tension is an important skill to acquire. The beadwork should feel flexible rather than floppy. A good gauge is to look at how much thread is showing. If the beads are able to slide on the thread, the tension is too soft. Pull your thread firmly after each stitch, holding the tip bead as you pull to enable the thread to draw up.

ingredients...

size 11° seed beads 10g each:

magenta opaque rainbow (A)
orange opaque rainbow (B)
matt bronze (C)

76 x4mm bicone crystals in two
colours: hyacinth, hyacinth 2xAB

clasp of your choice: or a copper
coloured sliding clasp with 3 loops.

Project three shows how to work an anchor row and place the stitches between anchor beads. It also shows how to add embellishment at the ends of the rows.

Foundation row
Use a stop bead, thread on 13 beads, alternating A and B.

Work the stalk and tip row
Pick up stalk beads 3xC, tip bead 1xA.
Pass back through 3xC and through two beads on the foundation row 1xB, 1xA. For the second and alternate stitches replace 3xC with 1x4mm crystal. Repeat to complete the row. Remove the stop bead, tie the working thread to the tail, then pass through to the tip bead of the last stitch.

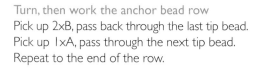

Start the spacer row
Pick up 2xB, pass back through the tip bead.
Turn the stalk so the thread is facing inward.
Place 1xB spacer beads between each tip bead to complete the row.

Turn, then work the anchor bead row
Pick up 2xB, pass back through the last tip bead.
Pick up 1xA, pass through the next tip bead.
Repeat to the end of the row.

Turn at the other end of the anchor row
Pass through the tip bead at the end of the row.
Pass through the lower of the 2xB, pick up 1xA, and pass through the upper of the 2xB to be in place to start the next stitch row.

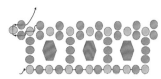

Start the next row

Pick up 3xC and 1xA. Pass back through 3xC.
Pass through the next anchor bead.
Adjust your beads so that the stitch fits
neatly between the two anchor beads.
Work the next stitch as 1x4mm (second
colour) 1xA. Alternate the two stitches
until the row is complete, ending with a
3xC, 1xA stitch.

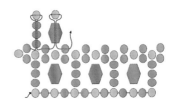

Turn at the end of the row

When the last stitch is completed, pass
through the upper of the 2xB beads at the
end of the row. Pick up 1xA, pass through
the lower of the 2xB then the tip bead
again. Pass up through the stalk and tip of
the last stitch to be in place to start the
next spacer bead row.

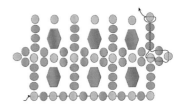

Finishing off

Keep working through the sequence of
rows, alternating the crystal colours for each
row, until the piece is the desired length.
End with a spacer bead row and attach the
clasp of your choice.
To attach a clasp, find the centre point of
the end of your bracelet (either a bead or
a space) stitch the centre loop of the clasp
here. Weave through to attach each of the
other two loops on the clasp.

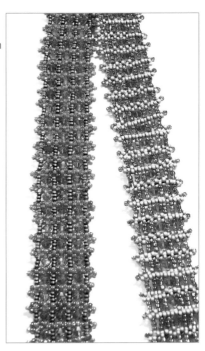

Crystal variation

The design shown on the right uses the
same pattern but just the centre stitch of
each row has a crystal stalk. All the other
stalks are worked in one colour of seed
bead. Tip, spacer and anchor beads are all
worked in a second colour.

...homespun vintage mix.

This mix is soft and easy, peachy orange, mustard, soft turquoises and richer shades of bronze and gun metal. It's a familiar and comfortable blend of faded peppery nasturtiums, galvanized garden tools, grandpa's cravat and hand knitted jumpers. A deliciously nostalgic, old fashioned, yet easy to wear mix of colours.

The first three projects used the basic stitch and introduced the different variations. Stitching over a foundation bead, adding anchor rows and stitching between anchor beads.

The following three projects introduce a new step which is to vary the stitch lengths within a row. In one row each stitch can be a different length which enables the creation of new patterns and new shapes.

The variations shown for the first three projects can all be applied to these new ones too.

Stitches can go from short to long, left to right, in a row. Try the Tea dance lariat, with a crystal nestling in the centre of each longest row.

Stitches can go from short to long and back again within a row, giving you a beautifully curved scallop shape. Make them in a repeating band as in the Sea curl bracelet.

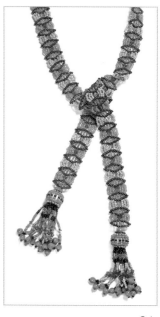

Stitches can also do the reverse, short to long and back, long to short and back. Mix the two rows to create a new pattern, as in the Egyptian eye lariat.

simple increases, link into a lariat...

A mix of softly coloured matt finish beads and gently gleaming crystals.
The Tea dance lariat is a simple sequence of increases, reversed for each row to create a sweet zig zag pattern of spacer bead rows. If crystals don't appeal, use softer matt accent beads. A size 8° seed bead to match the bead colours will look great and fit within the bead count given in the pattern.

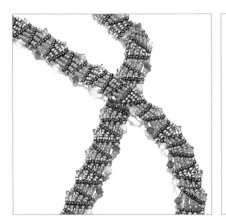

ingredients...

size 11° seed beads 15g each:
metallic bronze (A)
matt opaque turquoise (B)
matt opaque mustard (C)
frosted peach (D)
matt metallic grey (E)

68 x 4mm bicone crystals each in four colours to match the B - E seed beads

Fireline beading thread

Project four shows how to work stitches of different lengths within a single row. The stitches alternate from left to right on each row to form a zig zag pattern of tip and spacer beads. Each row is worked in one of four colours. All the tip and spacer beads are worked in a single colour (A).

Foundation row
Use a stop bead and thread on 9xA.

Work the stalk and tip row
Push all the beads down to the stop bead.
Pick up stalk 1xB, tip 1xA, pass back through 1xB, then through two beads on the foundation row.
Next stalk 2xB, next stalk 3xB, next stalk 4xB, last stalk 2xB, 1x4mm crystal, 1xB.

Work the spacer bead row
Weave through to the tip bead of the last stitch.
Pick up 1xA and pass through the next tip bead.
Repeat to the end of the row.

Work the following rows
Change to C beads and repeat the stitch sequence, with the 1xC, 1xA stitch above the longest stitch of the previous row. Add the next spacer bead row.
Work a row in each of the four colours, then repeat the colour sequence.

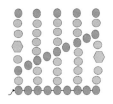

Finishing off
When your piece is a lariat length (about 90 - 120 cm) work a fringe from each of the stitches of the last row (then go back and do the same at the start), see picture left.

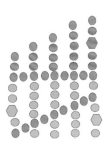

ingredients...

size 11° seed beads 15g each:

metallic gun metal (A)
clear rainbow turquoise (B)
frosted peach (C)
matt opaque turquoise (D)

68 x 4mm bicone crystals each in two
colours to match the B and C seed beads

28 x 6mm round accent beads
Fireline beading thread

The Egyptian eye lariat shows how to work with different length stitches in alternate rows. The first set of stitches are in a sequence from short to long and back again and are always worked in the same colours, A and B. For the second set of stitches the sequence is reversed. The second set rows alternate colours, C and D. The tip and spacer beads are all worked in A.

The ends of the lariat are decorated with beaded beads (see page 46), attached to the centre bead of each end row. The fringes are worked into the beaded bead. Each tassel is worked in a series of fringes with crystals and accent beads for embellishment. Use the photographs as a guide or create fringes with your own colour and bead sequence.

Foundation row
Use a stop bead and thread on 9xA.

Work the stalk and tip row A
Push all the beads down to the stop bead.
Pick up 1xB, 1xA, pass back through 1xB, then through the bead on the foundation row.
Pick up 2xA, pass through the tip bead of the stitch just worked, then the stalk, then through 2xA on the foundation row. Add the remaining stitches for the row in this sequence: next stalk 2xB, next stalk 3xB, next stalk 2xB, last stalk 1xB.

Turn at the end of the row
Complete the last stitch, then pick up 2xA, and pass through the tip bead of the last stitch worked. This mirrors the end embellishment added at the start of the row.

Work the spacer row and end embellishment

Place 1xA between each tip bead.
At the end of the row pass through the first
bead of the 2xA added at the start, pick up 1xA,
pass through the second of the 2xA.
Pass through all the beads of the foundation row and
the first bead of the 2xA at the other end.
Pick up 1xA, pass through the second bead and the
tip bead, to be in place to start the next stitch row.

Work the stalk and tip row B

Using C beads the first three stitches are worked
over adjacent beads of the new foundation
row - work over 1x tip, 1x spacer, 1x tip -
first stalk 6xC, second stalk 5xC, third stalk 4xC.
Pass through two beads to place the centre stitch,
stalk 1x4mm crystal.
Pass through two beads then work the remaining
three stitches. First stalk 4xC, second stalk
5xC, third stalk 6xC. Pass through to the tip of the
last stitch to be in place to add the spacer row.
Add 1xA between each tip bead.

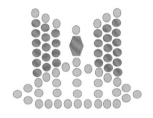

The row sequence

Continue by repeating the first row (A), always
worked in colours A and B. Then repeat the second
row (B), changing to colour D beads. The next first
row will be followed by a second (B) row worked
in C beads. The sequence is A rows separated by
B rows which themselves alternate in colour. Keep
working until there is a lariat length (90 - 120cm).

Finishing off

Make two beaded beads (see page 46). Work a fringe on to each bead of the last
row at one end of the beaded bead.
Attach a new thread to the centre bead on the end of your lariat, thread through
an accent bead, the beaded bead and another accent bead.
Pick up 1xA, pass back through the beads to the lariat.
Repeat to make sure your tassel is firmly attached then finish off the thread.
Repeat at the other end of the lariat.

ingredients...

size 11° seed beads 15g each:

matt teal (A)

transparent rainbow sea (B)

matt opaque turquoise (C)

clasp of your choice: *or use a metal press stud (snap fastener)*.

The Sea curl bracelet is made of sections. Each is worked from the edge of the previous section. Soft colour changes in sea blues add definition to the pattern. The curl section is formed with two types of increase.

Each row has a sequence of stitch lengths and an increased number of stitches.

Foundation row
Use a stop bead and thread on 9xA.

Work the stalk and tip row A
Push all the beads down to the stop bead.
Stitches are worked over each bead on the foundation row, pick up 1xB, 1xA, pass back through 1xB, then through one bead on the foundation row. Next stalk 1xB, next two stalks 2xB, next stalk 3xB, next two stalks 2xB, last two stalks 1xB.

Work the spacer bead row.
Weave through to the tip bead of the last stitch. Pick up 1xA, pass through the next tip bead. Repeat to the end of the row.

Work the next stalk and tip, and spacer rows B
Stitch over each bead of the previous row (tip and spacer beads).
First two stalks 1xB.
Next four stalks 2xB.
Next five stalks 3xB.
Next four stalks 2xB.
Last two stalks 1xB.
Step up through the last stitch and add 1xA between each tip bead.

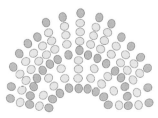

Anchor bead row

Place 1xB anchor bead over each tip bead of the previous row, passing through the spacer beads.

Weave through the beads

Weave through the edge row to the anchor bead second from the centre and bring the needle through this bead.

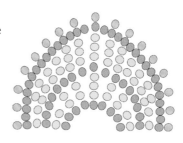

Add the new foundation row

Pick up 9xC and pass the needle through the anchor bead which lies second from centre on the other side.

Work the stalk, tip and spacer rows

Repeat the stitch sequence for the first stalk and tip row, using C beads for tips and B beads for stalks. At the end of the row, bring the needle through to the tip bead of the last stitch worked. Pick up 1xC, pass through the anchor bead next in line on the edge of the first section. Pass through the 1xC and tip again, then place 1xC between each tip bead. At the end of the row pick up 1xC and pass through the next anchor bead on the edge, the 1xC again, and the last tip bead.

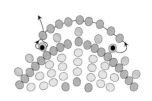

Work the next stalk, tip and spacer rows

Repeat the stitch sequence for the stalk, tip and spacer rows B. With the needle coming out of the last tip bead, pick up 1xC, pass through the same anchor bead as before, then through the 1xC and tip bead. Add 1xC between each tip bead, and repeat the step at the end of the row.

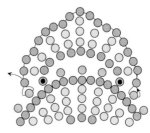

Anchor bead row

Place 1xB anchor bead over each tip bead of the previous row, passing through the spacer beads.

Finishing off

Work more sections, alternating the bead colour for each. When the piece is a bracelet length, work one more section with just the first stitch and spacer bead rows. Sew a press stud to one side of this smaller section. Sew the second part of the press stud to the centre bottom of the first section worked. The smaller section should fasten neatly under the first row of the larger section, to make an almost invisible join.

...Natural neutrals mix.

One of the most versatile palettes, natural neutrals can be any earthy shade from sun bleached stone, through sand, to terra-cotta and inky coal. Neutrals sit well together and get lively if you mix pale and dark tones. Accent colours can be any bright spot you like. French blue is a sophisticated addition.

Albion Stitch the next step...

The next step from the Sea curl project is to exploit the stitch increase variations to the full and get circular. The motifs remain flat and the patterns are created by increasing between the stitches with spacer beads and the occasional anchor bead row.

The basic stitch language on page 10 mentions that the foundation row can be a row of beads or a ring of beads. Projects so far have started from a foundation row. By working from a ring of beads the stitch can be worked as a flat circular stitch. To keep the design flat the stitch length and increases come into play.

The quick to make Cute buttons motif is a good project to start with. The simple motifs are worked separately and linked with strands of beads, to make a continuous band.

The Basket weave motif shows how to work a different increase and how to use colour to emphasise the pattern.

The Chain link pattern works from a much bigger foundation ring, and each section interlinks with the previous one to create a band that will move gracefully as you wear it. Try the projects and then experiment with your own variations.

simple circles, cute as a button...

The first circular Albion Stitch project uses a single row of two bead stitches which lie flat because the spacer beads are added in pairs. Make lots and link them together into an easy to wear lariat. For a shorter necklace just make fewer motifs and link them in the same way and adding a clasp to join the ends.

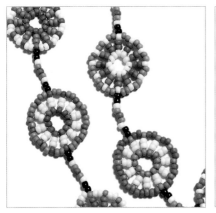

ingredients...

size 11° seed beads 15g each:

matt opaque blue (A)

matt opaque cream (B)

matt opaque rust (C)

5g shiny opaque black (D)

clasp of your choice: *for a shorter necklace, see below right.*

Foundation row
Thread on 12xA, tie the thread so the beads form a ring.

Work the stalk and tip row
Work a stitch over each bead on the foundation ring, stalk 2xC, tip 1xA. At the end of the round, bring the thread through to the tip of the first stitch worked.

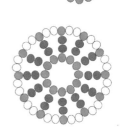

Add the spacer row
Place 2xB between each tip bead. Thread through all the beads again then finish off the thread tails.

Make more Cute button circles
Make 30 circles, changing the colours of the beads. For example, foundation ring B, stalk C, tip B, spacer A. There are six possible combinations (make five of each).

Finishing off
With a new thread, bring the needle out of a spacer bead next to a tip bead. Pick up a set of linking beads: 2xD, 1xB, 1xC, 1xA, 1xC, 1xB, 2xD. Pass the needle into a spacer bead next to a tip on a second circle. Thread through the edge beads of this circle to bring the needle out of the bead next to a tip directly opposite the join.

Repeat until all the circles are linked, then join the first to last in the same way.

Thread through the edge and linking beads, bringing your needle through to the spacer bead on the other side of the tip beads. This will centre the linking beads over the tip bead.

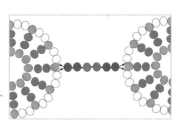

The Basket weave motif uses anchor bead rows to extend the increase variation.
By using dark and light toned beads in a simple sequence the pattern becomes a
striking contrast. Reverse the colours to create a very different pattern.
Link the motifs for a continuous necklace, or make a shorter version and add a clasp.

ingredients...

size 11° seed beads 15g each:
matt cream (A)
transparent toffee (B)
matt metallic bronze (C)
transparent rust (D)
shiny opaque black (E)

Size 8° seed beads 10g:
matt root beer (F)
18x 8mm pearls burgundy (P)

Foundation row
Thread on 12xA, tie the thread so the beads form a ring.

Work an anchor bead row
Place 1xA over each 1xA on the ring, passing through
the B beads. Bring the needle out of the first bead
added to step up.

Add the stalk and tip row
Place a stitch between each anchor bead of the previous
row, stalk 2xC, tip 1xB. Step up through the first stitch
worked in this row.

Add the spacer bead and anchor bead rows
Place three spacer beads between each tip bead, 1xA, 1xB,
1xA. Thread through the first set of spacer beads added
and bring the needle out of a B bead.
Add a row of anchor beads, 1xA over each A of the row
below, passing through the B beads. Finish off the thread tails.

Make more Basket weave circles
Make 17 more Basket weave circles, varying all the colours
except the A beads. There are six possible combinations.

Finishing off
The Basket circles are joined in the same way as the
button circles (see page 31). Link beads are:
1xF, 3xA, 1xF, 3xA, 1x P, 1xF, 3xA, 1xF, 3xA, 1xF.
Start from an anchor bead next to a stitch tip on the
circle edge. Join all the circles, then weave back through
to centre the link beads between the anchor beads.

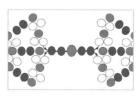

33

simple circles, linked together...

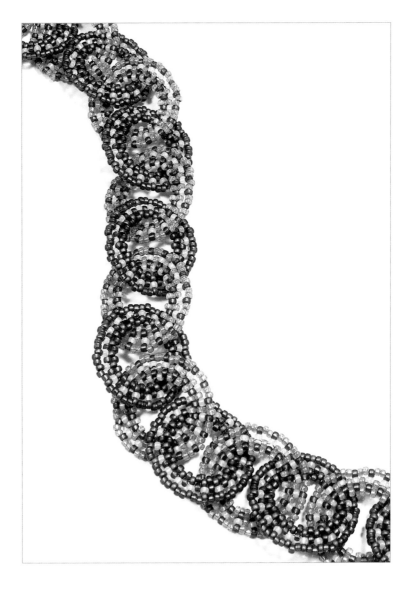

Chain link circles are joined together as they are worked. The internal diameter of each link allows plenty of movement, making this a slinky chain that will lie comfortably. The circles alternate in colour to add a simple pattern variation.

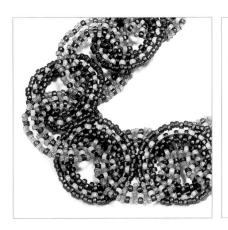

ingredients...

size 11° seed beads 15g each:

silver lined silky grey (A)
silver lined silky bronze (B)
silver lined silky straw (C)
matt metallic bronze (D)

Clasp of your choice: *or a bronze toggle and bar clasp*

Foundation row Link A
Thread on 38 beads alternating 1xA, 1xB. Tie the beads in a ring.

Add an anchor bead row
Bring the needle through a B bead, place 1xA over each 1xA on the ring, passing throught the B beads. Step up through the first A bead added.

Add the stalk and tip row
Place a stitch between each anchor bead, stalk 1xC, tip 1xB. Step up to the tip bead of the first stitch added.

Spacer bead row
Place 2xA between each tip bead of the previous row. Pass through all the beads of this row again, then finish off the thread tails.

Start the next link, link B
Pick up 38 beads alternating 1xB, 1xD. Pick up the first link and pass the thread through the centre hole, then tie the beads into a ring as before.

Add the anchor bead row
Place 1xB over each B bead in the ring, passing through the D beads.

Add the stalk and tip row
Place a stitch between each anchor bead, stalk 1xC, tip 1xD.

Spacer bead row
Place 2xB between each tip bead of the previous row, pass through all the beads of this row again, then finish off the thread tails.

Finishing off
Make links in the alternating colours until the piece is the desired length, ending with an A link. Attach your clasp to the outer edge of the first and last link.

inspired by the colours...

...summer fruits mix.

This vibrant mix is surprisingly easy to wear if you're not averse to some zingy colours. Think of a bowl of the juiciest citrus fruits like limes, oranges and pink grapefruits. Add the pure synthetic brights of plastic sandals, buckets and spades and fizzy drinks. Mix them all up together and you have a spirit-lifting beach babe mix.

36

Albion Stitch the next step...

The previous section shows how to work the stitch as flat circular motif.
The next development is to use this technnique without the increases and explore
the stitch in its tubular form. Make your first foray into three dimensions.

Tubular Albion Stitch is worked from a
foundation ring of beads but without
increases, the spacer bead rows pull in the
stitches so that they form an even tube.

Like each aspect of Albion Stitch, there are
always a myriad of variations to explore.
Tubular Albion Stitch is the one which will
accommodate changes in stitch lengths and
bead sizes most easily. Each row is a unit
in itself so each row can be worked in a
different combination of beads.

Tubular Albion Stitch can also be worked with
increases, in the same way that the circular
motif is formed. Increase the bead count
within the spacer bead rows, then add stitches over each tip and spacer bead,
rather than alternate ones. Increases can be gentle or extreme, which will change the
contours of the tube from straight sided, to gently undulating or radically shaped.

Tubular Albion Stitch is flexible, will bend well in any direction and is therefore ideal
for necklaces and bracelets.

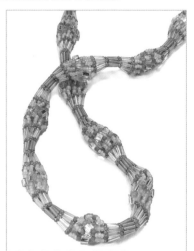

The Carnival tube is made using two stitch rows, one with seed bead stalks and one with a bugle bead stalk. The tip bead colours change for each row and the spacer beads are worked in the same colour as the tip beads. Work the rows in any sequence to create your own patterns within the tube.

ingredients...

size 11° seed beads 15g each:

shiny opaque yellow (A)
shiny opaque lime (B)
transparent magenta (C)
shiny opaque orange (D)

4mm bugle beads 15g frosted green (E)

Clasp: *this can be a continuous necklace or use a clasp of your choice.*

Foundation row
Thread on 16xA, tie the thread so the beads form a ring.

Work stalk and tip row A
Place a stitch over alternate beads on the foundation ring (8 stitches), stalk 1xE, tip 1xA. Bring the thread through to the tip of the first stitch worked.

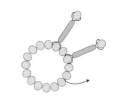

Add the spacer row
Place 1xA between each tip bead. Pass through a few beads again and pull tight to close the circle. Bring the needle out of a tip bead.

Work stalk and tip row B
Place a stitch over the spacer beads of the previous row (8 stitches), stalk 1xC, 1xD, 1xC, tip 1xB. To step up, bring the thread through to the tip of the first stitch worked.

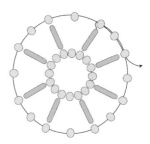

Add the spacer row
Place 1xB between each tip bead. Pass through a few beads again and pull tight to close the circle.

Finishing off
For the Carnival necklace the sequence - 3x stitch row A, 1x stitch row B, 3x stitch row A, 2x stitch row B, 1 x stitch row A, 2 x stitch row B - is repeated until the piece is long enough to slide over the head. To join the ends, work an additional row by passing the needle through the beads of the foundation row in place of adding a tip bead for the stitches.

The Carousel necklace is worked in three rows: a bugle bead row with a stitch over each foundation bead, a bugle bead row with spacer beads between the tips and a mixed bead row with spacer beads. The sequence is reversed to create the repeating pattern. Join the ends for a slide on necklace or add a clasp for a shorter version.

ingredients...

size 11° seed beads 15g each:
matt opaque coral (A)
frosted orange (B)

6mm bugle beads 15g each:
frosted aqua (C)
transparent rainbow lime (D)
size 8° seed beads 10g each:
dark and light pink (E)
3mm cube beads 15g silver lined lime

Foundation row
Thread on 9xA, tie the thread so the beads form a ring.

Work the stalk and tip row A
Place a stitch over each bead on the foundation ring, stalk 1xC, tip 1xA. Bring the thread through to the tip of the first stitch worked. Pass the thread through all the tip beads to draw them into a tight ring.

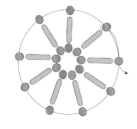

Work the stalk, tip and spacer row B
Place a stitch over each bead of the previous row, stalk 1xD, tip 1xB. Bring the thread through to the tip of the first stitch worked.
Place 1xB between each tip bead, pass through a few beads again and pull tight to close the circle.

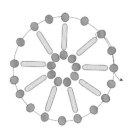

Work the stalk, tip and spacer row C
Place a stitch over each tip bead of the previous row, stalk 3xB, 1xE, 1x cube, 1xE, 3xB, tip 1xA. Bring the needle through to the tip bead of the first stitch worked, then link the tips with 1xA. Bring the needle out of a spacer bead.

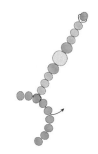

Work the stalk and tip row D
Work a stitch over each tip bead of the previous row, stalk 1xD, tip 1xB. Bring the thread through to the tip of the first stitch worked. Pass through all the tip beads to form a tight ring.

Repeat the row sequence until your piece is the desired length.
Join the last row (C) to the foundation row, or add a clasp of your choice.

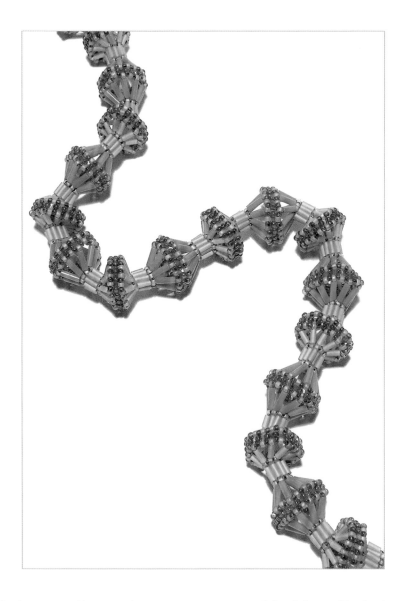

The Lantern necklace uses increases to create more defined shapes. The bugle beads hold the beadwork neatly in place. The row sequence is simple once you get started and the result is a light and airy colourful necklace that is easy to wear.

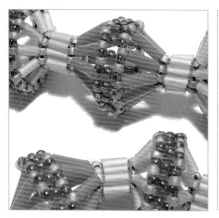

ingredients...

size 11° seed beads 15g each:
frosted green (A)
frosted orange (B)
transparent magenta (C)

4mm bugle beads 15g frosted lime (D)
7mm bugle beads 15g opaque orange (E)

Clasp of your choice: *or a magnetic ball shaped clasp*

Foundation row
Thread on 9xA, tie the thread so the beads form a ring.

Work the stalk and tip row A
Place a stitch over each bead on the foundation ring, stalk 1xD, tip 1xA.
Pass the thread through all the tip beads to draw them into a tight ring.

Work the stalk, tip and spacer row B
Place a stitch over each bead of the previous row, stalk 1xE, tip 1xB.
Place 1xB between each tip bead and pull tight to close the circle.

Work the stalk, tip and spacer row C
Place a stitch over each spacer bead of the previous row, stalk 1xC, tip 1xC.
Bring the needle through to the tip bead of the first stitch worked, then link the tips with 1xA. Bring the needle out of a spacer bead.

Work the stalk and tip row D
Place a stitch over alternate beads of the previous row, so the stalks line up with those of the B row, stalk 1xE, tip 1xA. Pass through all the tip beads to form a tight ring.

Repeat row A

Work the stalk, tip and spacer row E
Place a stitch over each bead of the previous row, stalk 1xD, tip 1xB.
Place 1xB between each tip bead and pull tight to close the circle.

Repeat row C

Work the stalk, tip and spacer row F
Work a stitch over the spacer beads of the previous row so the stalks line up with the stalks of the B row, stalk 1xD, tip 1xB. Pass through the tip beads to form a tight ring.

Repeat the row sequence until your piece is the desired length.
You may want to work a few A rows at each end, so the necklace will sit comfortably at the back. Attach the clasp of your choice.

inspired by the colours...

...Vintage spring mix.

The idea for this colour palette started with a love of Auricula flowers. They are such quaint and old fashioned flowers, grown for their dusty vintage colours. Lavender and primroses, faded prints on cotton dresses and that lovely gold edging on old tea services. This vintage spring mix is muted olive, violet, lilac, lemon and mustard, with a glint of gold thrown in as an accent.

44

Albion Stitch the next step...

Albion Stitch can be used in a slightly modified tubular form to cover shapes.
The stitches are the same as for flat linear, circular and tubular. The variation comes in
the use of spacer beads, or no spacer beads to shape the tubular form more, enabling it
to fit neatly around a spherical shape.

The following projects are worked over 12mm wooden beads. Simple increases
and decreases enable the beadwork to follow the contours of the wooden bead.

The variations for beaded beads are more
limited, as the stitch is at its best worked in one
size of seed bead. Once you understand the
technique, bead counts and stitch lengths can
be used to create very different effects.
Small increases in bead size can be
accommodated. Try size 10° triangles, or size 8°
seed beads, as shown in the following projects.

Fill in beads

The most basic beaded bead is the Fill in bead. These are a simplified
version of flat circular Albion Stitch. They are quick to make and add
instant texture and detail to any bead stringing project.
Experiment with other accent beads for the tips to add more detail.

beaded beads, with simple stringing...

The first beaded bead is worked in two different rows. A three bead stalk row spans the widest part of the base bead and two one stalk rows hug the ends. Simply strung with vintage style filigree end caps and pearls, this mustard and bronze mix will add elegant detail to any outfit.

ingredients...

size 11° seed beads 15g each:
matt opaque mustard (A)
metallic bronze (B)
colour lined green/gold (C)

19 x 12mm wooden beads
48 x 3mm pearls: olive
38 x filigree end caps

1g size 15° seed beads: clear
clasp of your choice: *or an antique
bronze toggle clasp*

Foundation row

Thread on 26xA, tie the thread so the beads form a ring.

Work the stalk and tip row A

Place a stitch over alternate beads on the foundation
ring, stalk 1xB, 1xA. Bring the thread through to the
tip of the first stitch worked.

Work the spacer row

Place 1xA between each tip bead. Pass through a
few beads once more, then place the wooden bead
into the collar of beads. Pull the thread up tight.
Knot the thread to secure this row if you need to.

Work the stalk and tip row B

Place a stitch over each tip bead of the previous row,
stalk 1xB, tip 1xA. Bring the needle through to the
tip bead of the first stitch worked. Pass through all
the tip beads and pull them into a tight ring.

Weave through to the foundation row

Repeat the stalk and tip row B. Pass through all the
tip beads and pull them into a tight ring, then finish off
the thread tails.

Finishing off

Make 19 beaded beads in total, changing the B for C on some of them.
To join the beads use Fireline thread and form a loop of 7x15° seed beads.
Pass the thread through a link in the clasp. Knot the thread then string on pearls,
seed beads and beaded beads using an end cap on each side of the beaded beads.
Finish off with a second loop of 7x15° beads and the other clasp section.

beaded beads, with rich pearls...

The second beaded bead uses one bead stalks with a slightly larger bead for the centre row of stitches. This method covers more of the surface of the wooden bead. More beaded beads and pearls will be needed for a larger bangle.

Thread the finished beads and pearls on to beading elastic. This fine, clear elastic is surprisingly strong and available under different brand names like 'Stretch Magic'.

For a bracelet with a clasp, simply string the beads and attach a clasp, adding an extra pearl to even things up so there is one at each end.

If pearls don't appeal, use any 10mm accent bead or add some Fill in beads to sit between the beaded beads, (see page 45).

ingredients...

size 11° seed beads 15g each:
silver lined violet (A)
silver lined lilac (B)

size 10° triangle beads 10g:
transparent lilac (C)

8 x 12mm wooden beads*
9 x 10mm x filigree end caps*

Elastic for threading
* makes a 7cm inner diameter bracelet

Foundation row

Thread on 28 beads alternating A and B, tie the thread so the beads form a ring. Bring the thread out of a B bead.

Work an anchor row

Pick up 1xA, pass through the next B bead on the ring, repeat to the end then step up through the last B bead on the ring and the first A bead added for this row.

Work the stalk and tip row A

Stitches are worked between anchor beads of the previous row, stalk 1xC, tip 1xB. Bring the thread through the tip bead of the first stitch worked to step up.

Work the spacer bead row

Place 1xA between each tip bead of the previous row. Place the wooden bead in to the collar of beads and then pull the thread up tight.

Repeat the anchor row

Work the stalk and tip row B

Stitches are worked between the anchor beads of the previous row, stalk 1xA, tip 1xB. Repeat to the end then step up to the tip bead of the first stitch worked. Pass through all the tip beads to form a tight ring. Weave through to the foundation row, and repeat the stalk and tip row B. Finish off the thread tails.

Finishing off

Cover all the wooden beads in the same way. Thread the 10mm pearls and beaded beads alternately on to beading elastic. Knot the elastic firmly.

beaded beads, with pattern and texture...

This design uses two patterns of beaded beads and Fill in beads to add texture between them. Use 15g each of size 11° and size 15° seed beads in violet to make the Fill in beads (see pattern on page 45), the project shown uses 28 x Fill in beads. The beaded beads are a mix of long and short stalks, and use a range of bead sizes. Thread the beads on to Fireline, following the instructions on page 47.
Allow a short strand of 8°s and 11°s at each end, so the necklace sits comfortably.

ingredients...

size 11° seed beads 15g each:
colour lined lemon (A)
frosted olive (B)
colour lined rainbow pale green (C)

10g size 8° seed beads; frosted olive (D)
10g size 10° triangle beads: straw (E)
1g size 15° seed beads: clear

21 x 12mm wooden beads
clasp of your choice: *or an antique silver toggle clasp*

Bead 1: Foundation row
Thread on 28xA. Tie the thread so the beads form a ring.

Work the stalk and tip row A
Place a stitch over alternate beads of the foundation row, stalk 1xE, 1xD, 1xE, tip 1xA.

Work the spacer row
Place 1xA between each tip bead. Pass through a few beads once more, then slide the wooden bead into place. Pull the thread up tight.

Work the stalk and tip row B
Place a stitch over each tip bead of the previous row, stalk 1xB, tip 1xC.
Bring the needle through to the tip bead of the first stitch worked. Pass through all the tip beads and pull them into a tight ring.

Weave through to the foundation row
Repeat the stalk and tip row B. Pass through all the tip beads and pull them into a tight ring, then finish off the thread tails.

Bead 2: Foundation row
Thread on 28 beads alternating A and B, tie the thread so the beads form a ring.
Bring the thread through an A bead.

Work the stalk, tip and spacer row A
Place a stitch over the A beads on the foundation ring, stalk 1xC, tip 1xA. Bring the thread through to the tip of the first stitch worked. Place 1xB between each tip bead. Repeat this row 2 more times, then slot the wooden bead in to place.

Work the stalk and tip row B
Place a stitch over each tip bead of the previous row, stalk 1xC, tip 1xB. Bring the needle through to the tip bead of the first stitch worked. Pass through all the tip beads and pull them into a tight ring. Weave through to the foundation ring and repeat this row. Finish off the thread tails.

inspired by the idea...

Inspired by an old crochet throw worked in a riot of colour by an unknown hand, I made this giant beaded bead necklace. Black is a great anchor colour for bright colours. In this beaded bead chapter I've shown that bead stringing and necklace making is a great way to show off beaded beads. It is also a nice way to add in accent beads of different sizes and textures.

more ideas to explore...

This oversize multi colour beaded bead necklace is worked over selection of wooden beads painted red, with diameters ranging from 15 to 25mm.

For the smaller sized bead a stitch row spans the widest part of the bead, with the foundation row and spacer row either side. To work out a foundation row, pick up an even number of beads and test it on the wooden bead. Simple but guaranteed. Next, check the stitch length, two or three beads are sufficient to span the gap. The following rows are also created by experimentation, with a two bead stalk row and a one bead spacer row, followed by a one bead stalk row with no spacers.

The middle sized beads are worked slightly differently. The first two have a foundation row which spans the exact centre of the wooden bead, with two bead stalk rows to either side. The following spacer row alternates between one bead and no bead, and the final row has no spacer beads.

The second two middle sized beads have a foundation row off set from the centre with an anchor bead row, reflected at the other side of the central two bead stalk row. The anchor beads allow an additional increment.

The following two rows are worked in the same way as the other middle sized beads, a spacer row with alternate one bead, no bead spacing, and a final row with no spacer beads.

The largest beads have a foundation row which spans the circumference of the bead and an anchor row. Three two bead stalk rows are needed to reach the edge of the wooden bead with first a one bead spacer row, then an alternating, one bead, no bead spacer row and no spacers for the last row.

Playing and experimenting are all that's needed to cover any form with Albion Stitch.

The giant necklace is finished with ready made crochet beads (nice and light), which are slightly squashy too, so they nestled into the big holes of the wooden beads. Use an over sized clasp to balance the scale of the beaded beads.

inspired by the colours...

...antique metals mix.

Like the neutral palette, the antique metal palette is accessible and easy to wear.
Think of verdigris, pewter, old bronze and antique silver then add the worn and
weathered shades of old leather. The range of beads in this colour palette is vast,
varied and delicious. It is almost impossible to get this mix wrong. For accent
colours add a dash of rich vermillion, viridian or pale alabaster.

54

Albion Stitch the next step...

The next step with Albion Stitch is to create pattern and shape within the stitches. This is the section that explores 'filigree'. It is the stepping stone to a whole world of new ideas. This development brings togther the various elements of Albion Stitch to enable the creation of more detailed patterns. The new element is thread direction which can change often within a piece.

The designs in this section show how to create single motifs that can be linked together and how to create motifs that are spun out in a continuous flow.
This is a completely new development for patterned beadwork and one with plenty of opportunity for experimentation.

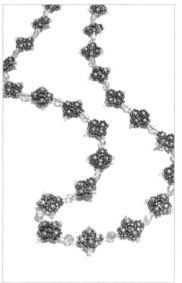

New variations can be made by changing stitch lengths, counts and definitely by experimenting with bead types and sizes.

Try the techniques and discover how to create filigree patterns. The colours of antique metals work well with these intricate designs.
Soft shades of grey and silvery gold make this colour mix wearable for day as well as evening.

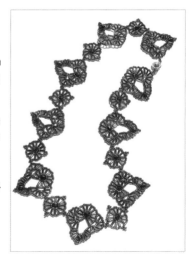

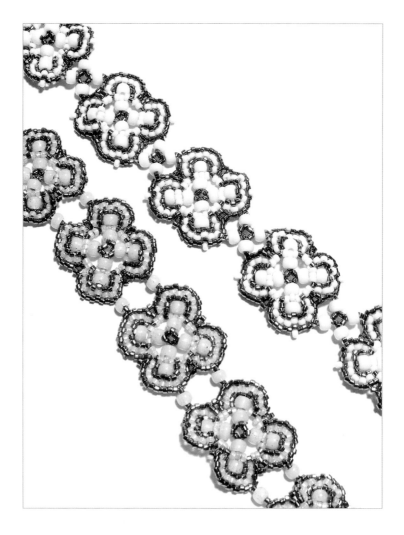

Elizabethan panes are made as individual pieces, linked together to complete the design. Link the panes as in the grey sample above, with 1xA, 1xC, 1xA, positioned over edge beads in the same way that the circle motifs were linked on pages 30 and 32. Alternatively, make smaller panes by working the foundation and first stalk and tip rows. Link two tips to one finished pane, and two to the next as in the cream sample above. Attach the clasp to the two end panes.

ingredients...

size 11° cylinder beads 15g:
galvanised tarnished silver (A)

size 11° seed beads 15g:
silky grey (B)

size 6° seed beads 15g:
silky grey (C)

clasp of your choice: *or a silver
magnetic sliding clasp with 2 loops.*

Foundation row
Thread on 8xA, tie the thread so the beads form a ring.

Work the stalk and tip row A
Place a stitch over alternate beads on the foundation ring,
stalk 1xC, tip 1xB. Bring the thread through
to the tip of the first stitch worked.

Work the spacer row
Place 1xB, 1xA, 2xB, 1xA, 1xB between each tip bead.
Bring the needle out of a tip bead of the previous row.

Work the stalk and tip row B
Place a stitch over each tip bead of the previous row,
stalk 1xC, tip 1xA. Bring the thread through a 1xB of the
previous row.

Create a new foundation row*
Pick up 4xA, pass through the 1xA tip bead, pick up 4xA,
pass through the 1xA on the other side of the stalk and tip.
Pass back through the last bead added.

Work the new stalk, tip and spacer row C
Place a stitch over each bead of the foundation row,
stalk 1xB, tip 1xA (9 stitches). Pass through the B bead
of the previous row. Pick up 1xA, then add 1xA spacer
between each tip bead. Pick up 1xA then weave through
to start the next set.** Repeat from * to ** three times.

Linking the panes together
As each pane is linked (see left), add 1xB over the centre
tip bead of each C row and 1xB to link the 3rd bead from
the base of each C row (see photo left).

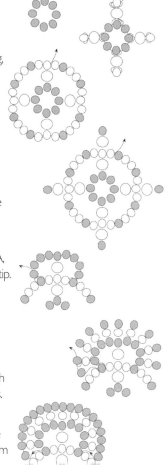

The Cloister ribbon is very simple to work, each motif is linked to the next and is worked in a continuous band. Its an addictive process.

Work with bigger beads may require an increase in the number of beads used to span the gap between the tip and foundation row beads. Gaps can also be filled with more embellishment by threading through the outer beads and placing crystals in the spaces above the A beads that link to the foundation ring.

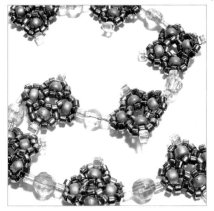

ingredients...

size 11° cylinder beads 15g:
metallic bronze (A)

size 8° seed beads 15g:
matt metallic khaki (B)

1.8mm cube beads 15g:
clear colour lined gold (C)

30-50 4mm round facet crystals:
grey rainbow finish (D)

Foundation row

Thread on 8xA, tie the thread so the beads form a ring.

Work the stalk and tip row A

Place a stitch over alternate beads on the
foundation ring, stalk 1xB, 1xA. Bring the thread
through to the tip of the first stitch worked.

Work a new foundation row

Pick up 3xA, pass through 1xA on the foundation
ring and the last bead added.
Pick up 3xA, pass through the next tip bead.
2nd and 4th tips only:- Pick up 1xC pass back
through tip bead.
Repeat until you are back at the first tip bead.

Work the linking section

Pick up 1xC, 1xD, 1xC, 1xA. Pass back through
the first three beads, the tip bead you started from
and then back through the four new beads. Pick up
1xB 1xA, pass back through 1xB, the 1xA tip of the
previous set of beads and both new beads again.

Work a new foundation row

Pick up 7xA and pass through the 1xA tip bead.
Pass through 4xA of this new ring of beads to be in
place to start adding the new stalk and tip row A.

Finishing off

Continue until the piece is the desired length then
add a small clasp for a shorter necklace or tie the
ends for a lariat length.

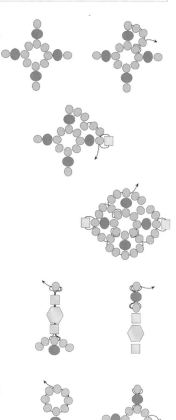

The Coined arch necklace uses the method of changing direction to make more complex motifs. Keep it simple with one colour of beads throughout, adding an accent colour with the crystals. Each motif is made separately then linked together alternating the arch and coin motifs.

With this more complex motif just follow the steps in sequence and it will begin to take shape. The second one will be quicker to make once you have mastered the technique.

ingredients...
size 11° cylinder beads 15g:
metallic bronze (A)

3mm bugle beads 15g:
metallic bronze (B)

26-32 x 4mm round facet crystals 15g:
metallic pewter (C)

clasp of your choice: *or a bronze snap together clasp.*

Arch motif foundation row
Thread on 12xA, tie the thread so the beads form a ring. Pick up 1xC and pass through a bead on the foundation ring to settle the C bead in to place.

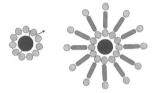

Work the stalk and tip row A
Place a stitch over each bead on the foundation ring, stalk 1xB, tip 1xA. Bring the thread through to the tip of the first stitch worked.

Work the spacer row
Place 2xA between each tip bead except the first and last. This will create a gap in the ring.

Add a new foundation row
Pick up 7xA, pass through the 6th bead from the end of the previous row, then through the last bead added.

The new beads fold backwards along the edge of the previous row. The following stitches will form the first of two half moon shapes which sit either side of the gap created in the spacer bead row.

Work the stalk and tip row B
Place a stitch over each bead of the new foundation row, stalk 1xB, tip 1xA. Bring the thread through to the tip of the last stitch added. The thread is now in place to add the spacer bead row.

Add the spacer bead row

Place 2xA between each tip bead. Add 2xA after the last tip bead then pass through the 10th bead on the edge. Thread through all the beads on the edge of the base to bring the thread out of the last tip bead at the other side of the gap.

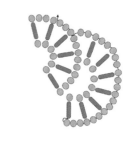

Repeat the steps

Repeat the steps to create a second half moon section to lie along the edge before the gap. At the end of the spacer bead row, pass back through the beads to bring the thread out of the tip bead as shown.

Add a new foundation row

Thread on 9xA and pass through the tip bead of the first half moon section, then through the last bead added.

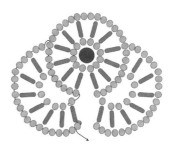

Work the stalk and tip row C

Place a stitch over each bead of the new foundation row.
First four stitches, stalk 1xB.
Fifth stitch, stalk 1xC.
Last four stitches, stalk 1xB.
Bring the thread through to the tip of the last stitch worked.

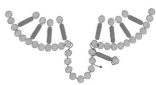

Work the spacer bead row

Pick up 1xA. Pass through the 4th bead from the edge of the base row, the 1xA and the tip bead again. Place 1xA between the tips of the next 3 stitches. Place 2xA before and 2xA after the tip of the centre stitch, then 1xA between the remaining tips. At the end of the row, thread on 1xA and pass through the 4th bead from the edge of the base row. Thread back through all the beads to the spacer bead before the centre tip bead. Thread on 3xA, then pass through the spacer bead after the tip bead. Thread through the edge beads, then finish off the thread tails.

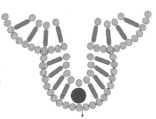

Coin motif foundation row

Thread on 12xA, tie the thread so the beads form a ring. Pick up 1xC and pass through a bead on the foundation ring to settle the C bead in to place.

Work the stalk and tip row A

Place a stitch over each bead of the foundation ring and then bring the thread out of the tip of the last stitch worked.

Work the spacer row

Place 3xA between the first and second tip bead. Place 2xA between the next two tip beads. Repeat until you are back at the start. The diagram shows the 3xA in a slightly darker shade. There will be four sets of 3xA separated by two sets of 2xA.

Work the embellishment row

Bring the thread through a centre bead of a set of 3xA. Thread on 3xA and pass back through the centre bead. Weave through to the next centre bead and repeat until you have 3xA sitting over each centre bead of the 3xA sets added in the previous round.

Finishing off

Make nine arch motifs and eight coin motifs.

Work from a centre bead of the embellishment beads on the coin edge, thread through the 3rd tip bead from the top of the half moon motif on the edge of an arch section. Weave through to the centre bead on the other side of the coin section, then link the next arch section. Repeat until all the motifs are linked, starting and finishing with an arch motif. Attach a clasp of your choice to the edges of these motifs.

Conclusion

The basic elements of Albion Stitch are now at your command.
From flat linear, through round, tubular, beaded bead and filigree.
These are the language of Albion Stitch. With them you can generate an endless and delicious range of patterns and designs. Variations are created by changing the ingredients within the recipes; the stitch lengths, bead sizes, spacer and anchor stitch rows. The other variation which I love to play with and which can dramatically change a piece is colour. The inspiration pages scattered through the book are designed to tempt you to experiment too.

Once you are comfortable with the basic language of Albion Stitch the story will continue in book two. Here the emphasis is on structure and form, and you will see how infinitely versatile the elements of Albion Stitch can be.
The projects incude bezels to capture treasures, sculptured
and rippling forms and three dimensional pieces.
Thank you for joining me to explore Albion Stitch and join me again in book two.

About the Author

Heather Kingsley-Heath has an Honours degree in Surface Pattern Design and first worked in the textile industry as a print designer, making jewellery and many other crafts in her free time. Heather moved into the publishing industry as a magazine editor before returning to the freelance life.

Heather started the Useful Booklet Company to produce booklets that are ideal for beginners who need to know how different beadwork techniques work. More books have followed, and a series of worksheets based on her popular classes.

To find out more about Heather's range of books, products, kits and worksheets please feel welcome to visit:

www.heatherworks.co.uk

To see more of Heather's creative work and commissions visit :

www.kingsley-heath.com